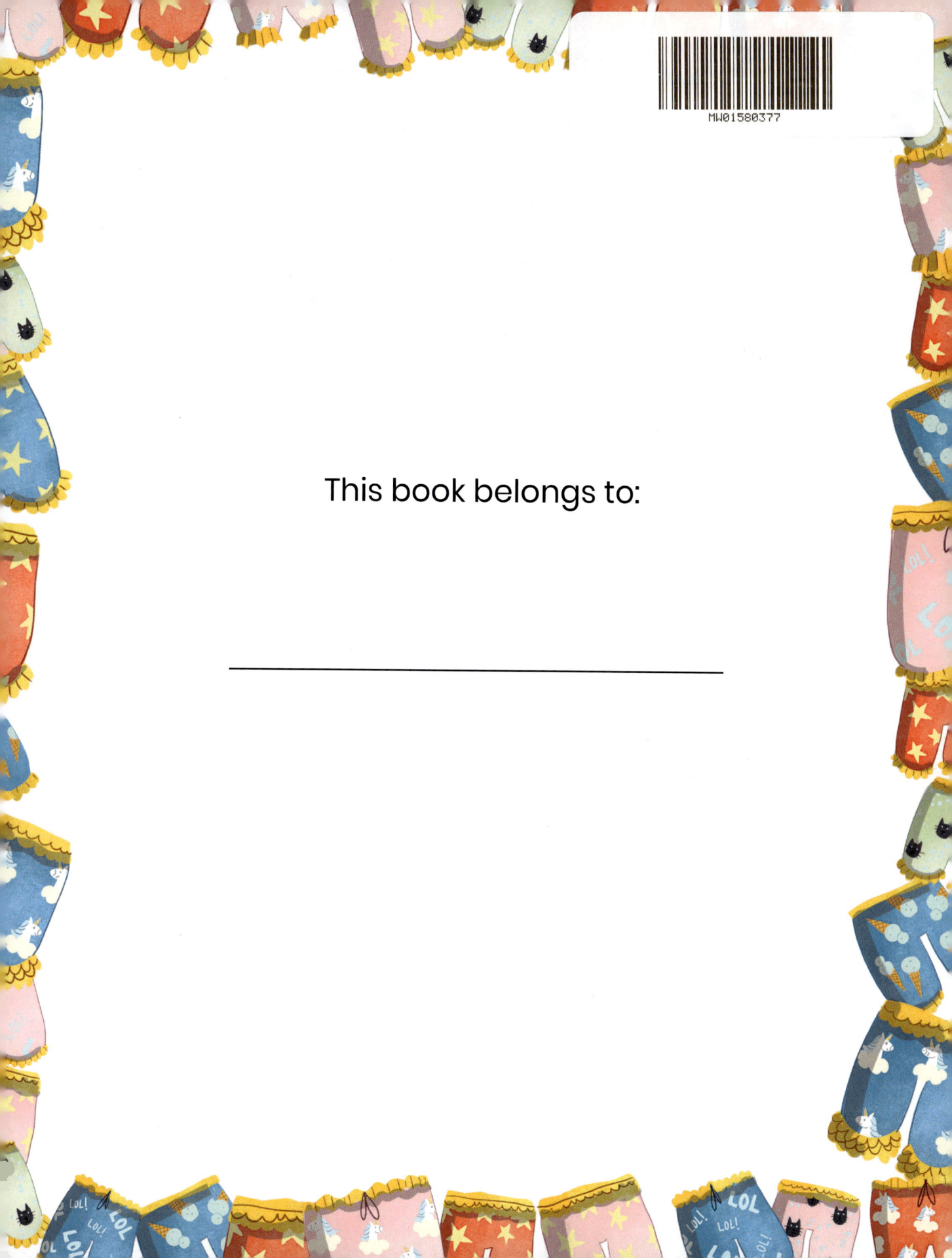

This book belongs to:

_____

Dressed in the Best!

Katie Pye · Rodrigo Paulo

Remember the tale
of the emperor's shame?
How he'd prance in his finery,
seeking great fame?
How two tailors well-tricked him
and made him believe
that the 'clothes' they had made
were a special new weave?
You'll have heard that he strutted
about quite undressed,
but...there's more to this story
than you might have guessed!

One day the vain emperor, modelling his clothes,
was prancing around when he suddenly froze.
"He's got nothing on!" blurted out a stunned child.
The emperor spun round incredibly wild.
He glared at the boy, "Don't speak rubbish to me!
I know what I'm wearing - that clearly can't be!"

Annoyed and impulsive, he stormed back inside,
"This clothing has promise! Let's take it world-wide!
Staff, go find those tailors! Have more of this made!
Then plan a great banquet where they'll be displayed.
I'll send a free gift to each noteworthy guest.
Then they can show off being... **dressed in the best.**"

The horses were sent and the invites received.

The noteworthy guests wondered what to believe!

Delighted, the gift had been quickly untied.
But baffled,

they found there was
nothing
inside!

Dearest Guest,

Please join me next month for a banquet. I will be displaying my new line of clothing. Please wear the gift I am sending you.

Kindest regards,
Emperor Boxham

Dearest Emperor Boxham,

Your wonderful joke had us laughing all day. We very much look forward to enjoying more of your humour at the banquet!

With warm regards,
King and Queen Shewsberry

Dearest Emperor Boxham,

Thank you for your kind invitation. I recently purchased a new outfit, which I will wear for the special occasion.

Best regards,
Duke Griffin

Dearest Emperor Boxham,

We were delighted to receive your invitation and accept with thanks.

Your gift was not enclosed in the box!

Yours sincerely,
King and Queen Wheaten

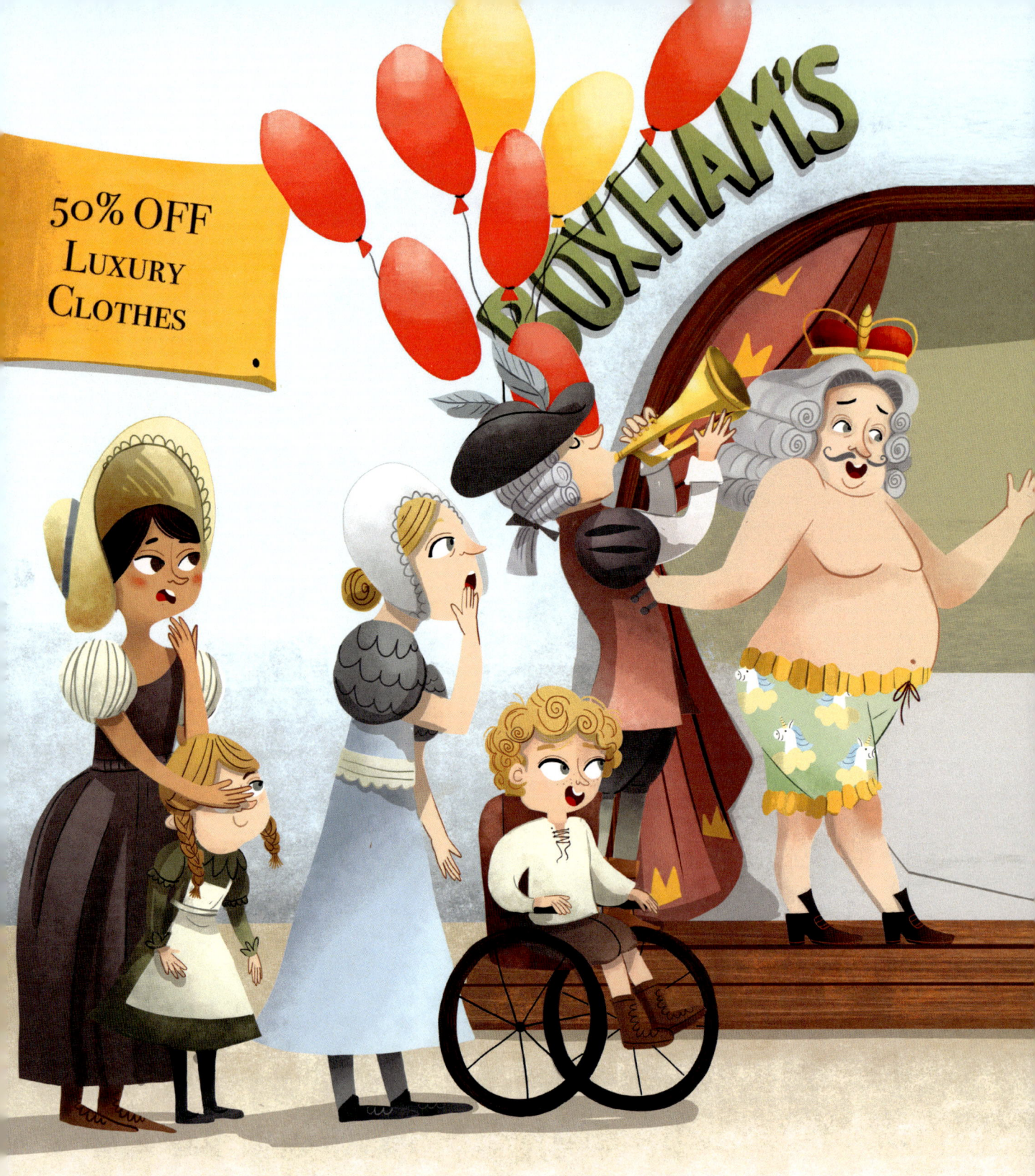

The emperor, stubborn, and sure he was right,
shrugged off the replies as he worked day and night.

He launched his first shop with a great jamboree,
then beamed at his staff, "You can all dress like me!"

Aghast, all the staff came together that night
and secretly schemed how to end their sad plight.
They knew that he'd listen to no one but he,
so...

    they made up a plan
           so he'd see what they see.

Once more,
 but in secret,
  a note went to guests;

a plea from his staff
with some shocking requests.

The emperor, hosting the feast the next day, invited his guests to enjoy his display.

"This breathtaking clothing that makes you all stare,
draws gasps at a glance and I just had to share!
As well as great clothing, the best to be seen,
I welcome you now to enjoy my cuisine!"

The guests shared a wink as they each took their seat.
Unseeing, the emperor cried, "Time to eat!"
The covers were lifted. The guests feigned delight.
BUT...

    not the poor emperor, stunned at the sight.

Confused and upset, he thought, "How can this be? How can they see something that I can not see?"

His stomach was growling, his mind was perplexed.
He slumped to his chair wondering what to do next.
It's then that the emperor finally spied -
his plate cover had a note hidden inside.

Dear Emperor
You have no clothes on!
Get dressed!
From Charlie

Then gasping, he noticed his body felt bare.
He looked down and now he just saw...

UNDERWEAR.

He mouthed, "I was wrong" and went red in the face, and raced from the banquet in utter disgrace.

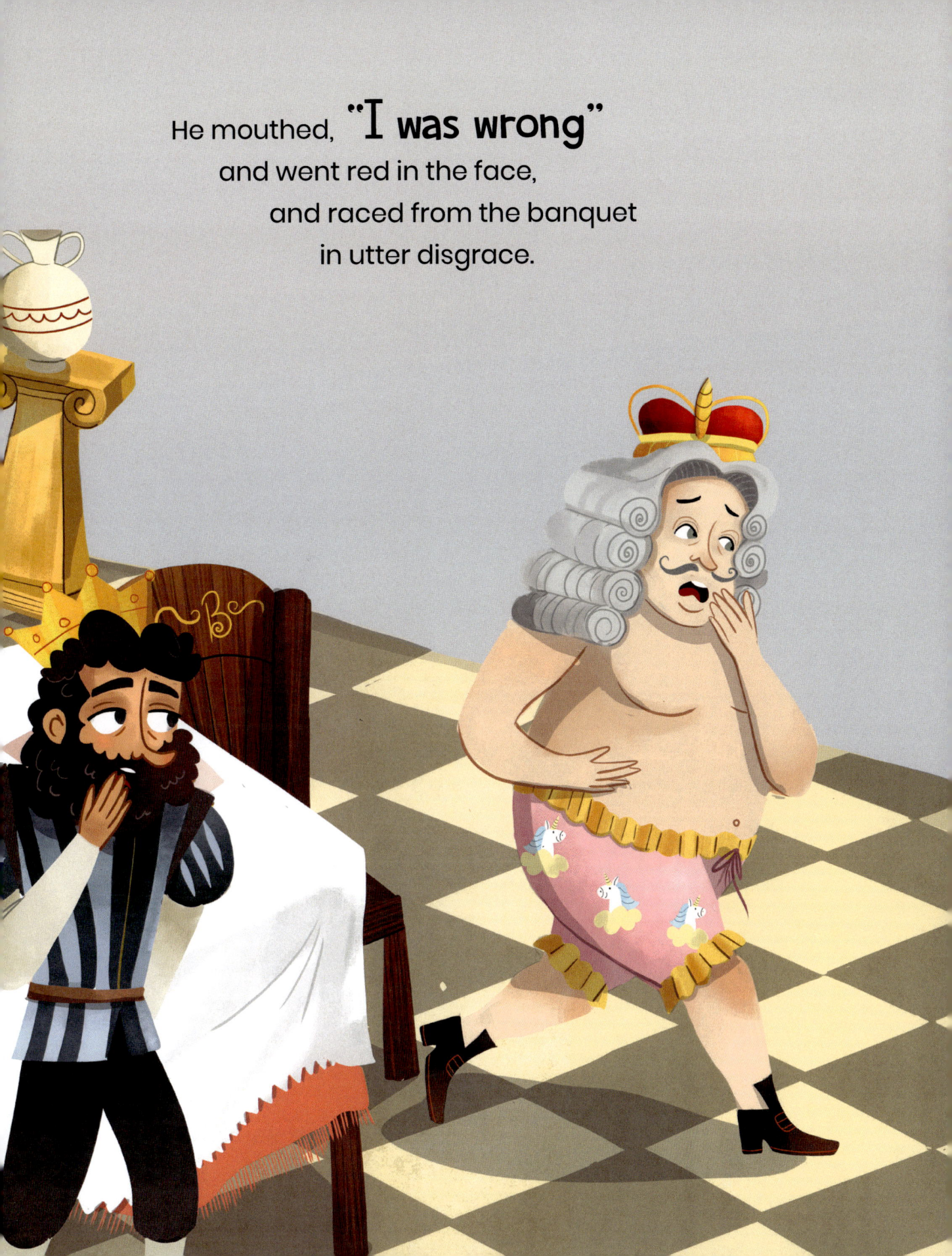

Well-humbled, the emperor learnt on that night -

to never

assume it is

him

that is right.

But to his great credit, he rallied once more.
His noteworthy guests, once again, were sent for...

Dearest Guests,

I'd like to invite you to another banquet – this time with food!

I am sending you a gift so that you too can be dressed in the best! Feel free to wear it at the party.

Kindest regards,
Emperor Boxham

P.S. Just kidding!

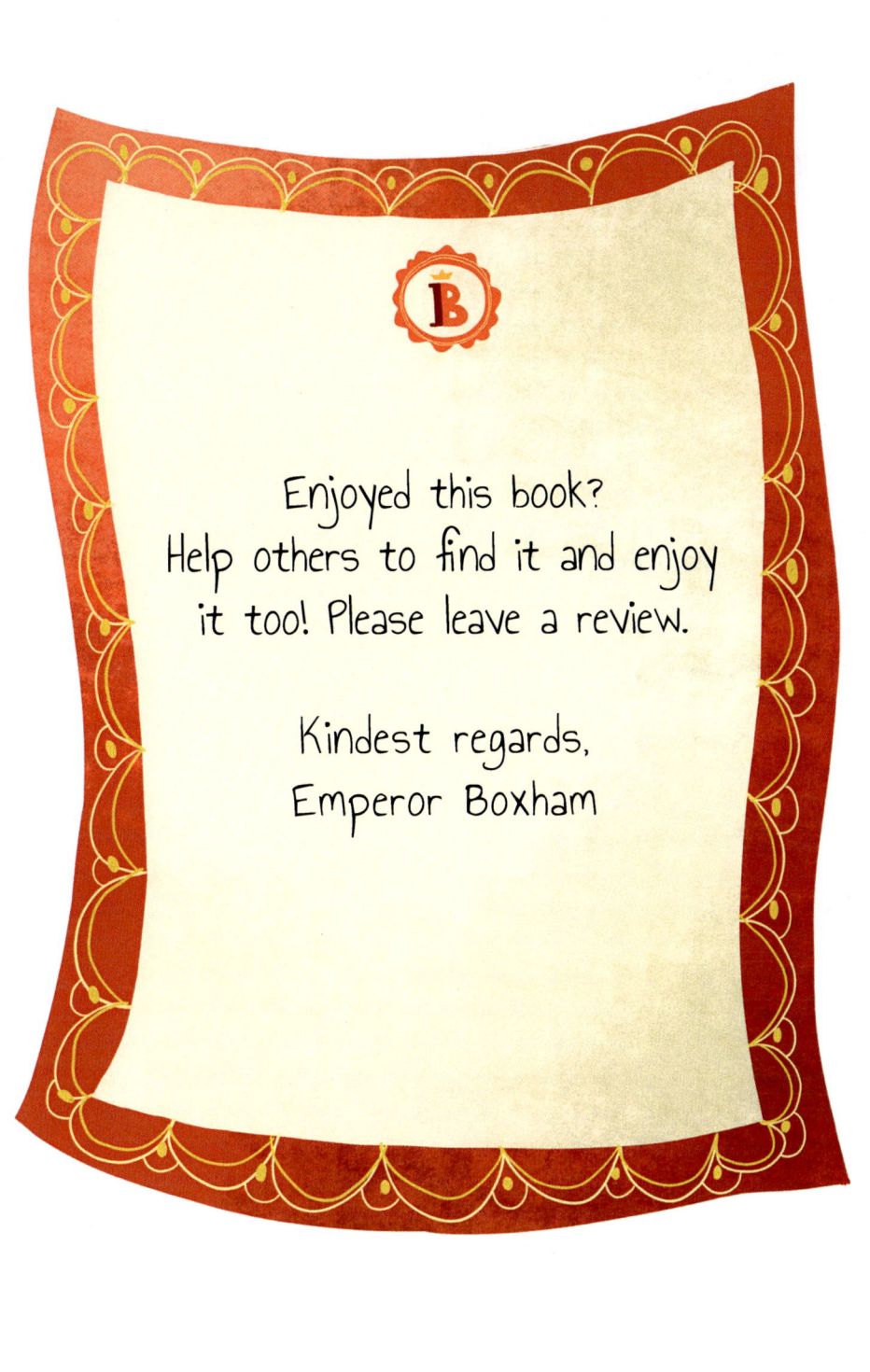

BEHIND THE SCENES

Why do you think I found it hard to listen and learn? Do you?

What do you think you have learnt that could help others?

If you could get all the help you need to do something you dream of, what would it be?

ACT ON IT!

- Choose a challenge. Brainstorm any help you need to complete the challenge! Get started this week!

- Create a different ending to the story and share it on www.fairytalefraud.com.

HOW TO BE A LEARNER...AND LIKE IT!

- Keep your goal in mind! Being a learner helps you reach it.
- Give yourself breaks! Do something fun!
- Have fair expectations. Everyone fails!
- Challenge 'I can't' thinking and get a support team!
- Ditch comparing. You'll get it in your time.
- Take small steps and celebrate success.

MEMORY MOTTOS

Nobody knows everything! Remember these when you find it hard to be a learner:

- Taking advice isn't being weak. It is making me stronger!
- Every person in the world is a learner – not just me.
- Just because I don't know, it doesn't mean that I can't.

Access more 'Behind the Scenes' materials free on
www.fairytalefraud.com

MORE FAIRYTALE FRAUD EXPOSED

Create even more conversations with your children with our growing Fairytale Fraud series.

Check out **www.fairytalefraud.com** for the range of topics, as well as free resources.

Create conversations about:

Gratitude

Trip Trap Trouble
(Billy Goats Gruff)

Managing Conflict

Sibling Wars
(Hansel and Gretel)

Healthy Habits

Ready for Rescue?
(Rapunzel)

Coping with Change

Breaking News!
(Humpty Dumpty)

Healthy Grief / Social Media

The Lost Years
(Sleeping Beauty)

Considering Others

Jack's Giant Problem
(Jack and the Beanstalk)

...and many more!

To Ariana, I am so proud to be your mum. You bring so much sunshine to the world and to my life.
Eternal love, Mum

Text copyright © 2020. Katie Pye
Illustrations copyright © 2020. Rodrigo Paulo
"The author exerts their ownership of this work under the NZ Copyright Act 1994. No part of this work may be copied, published or sold without the author's permission."
Published by HeadStart Thinking, Nelson, NZ.
ISBN 978-0-473-51634-5 (Soft cover) | 978-0-473-51635-2 (Hardcover)
978-0-473-51636-9 (Epub) | 978-0-473-51637-6 (Kindle) | 978-0-473-51638-3 (PDF)

Made in the USA
Coppell, TX
21 May 2025

49682958R00021